Red
Lips

Red Lips
Connie Gault

Red Lips
first published 2002 by
Scirocco Drama
An imprint of J. Gordon Shillingford Publishing Inc.
© 2001 Connie Gault

Scirocco Drama Editor: Glenda MacFarlane
Cover design by Terry Gallagher/Doowah Design Inc.
Author photo by Don Hall
Printed and bound in Canada

We acknowledge the financial support of The Canada Council for the Arts and the Manitoba Arts Council for our publishing program.

All rights reserved. No part of this book may be reproduced, for any reason, by any means, without the permission of the publisher. This play is fully protected under the copyright laws of Canada and all other countries of the Copyright Union and is subject to royalty. Changes to the text are expressly forbidden without written consent of the author. Rights to produce, film, record in whole or in part, in any medium or in any language, by any group amateur or professional, are retained by the author.
Production inquiries should be addressed to:
Connie Gault
cgault@accesscomm.ca

Canadian Cataloguing in Publication Data

Gault, Connie, 1949-
    Red Lips
A play.
ISBN 1-896239-88-9
    I. Title.
PS8563.A8445R43 2002 C812'.54   C2002-900246-X
PR9199.3.G374R43 2002

J. Gordon Shillingford Publishing
P.O. Box 86, 905 Corydon Avenue, Winnipeg, MB Canada R3M 3S3

Acknowledgements

I want to acknowledge the assistance of the following organizations and individuals in the development of this play:

- the Saskatchewan Playwrights' Centre, board, staff and actors and the Saskatchewan Arts Board and Regina Arts Commission, who make the SPC festival, readings and workshops possible

- the Goodman Theatre, Chicago, participating in "Above the Line," a New Canadian Play Development Symposium, sponsored by the Canada Council for the Arts, the Department of Foreign Affairs and International Trade and the Canadian Consulate

- the 2000 Banff playRites Colony—a partnership between the Canada Council for the Arts, The Banff Centre for the Arts, and Alberta Theatre Projects

- Alberta Theatre Projects, Bob White, Paula Danckert, the designers and the cast at A.T.P. for the first production—and especially Dennis Fitzgerald for his heroic Statue

- D.D. Kugler and my other readers and advisers: Gord Gault, Marlis Wesseler and Dianne Warren.

Connie Gault

Connie Gault lives in Regina, Saskatchewan. She is the author of several plays for stage and radio, including *Sky, The Soft Eclipse* and *Otherwise Bob* (Scirocco Drama, 1999). Her second short story collection, *Inspection of a Small Village*, published by Coteau Books, won the City of Regina Book Award. Her stories have appeared in anthologies such as the *Oxford Book of Stories by Canadian Women, Turn of the Story: Canadian Short Fiction on the Eve of the Millenium, The Writer's Path* and *Best Canadian Stories*.

Characters

JANIE: in her forties
KY/TRUE: forties
SARAH/NORMA: forties
WAITER: could be any age
GUARD/CHARLIE/STATUE/DINER: forties
OLD WOMAN/ROSE/MYRTLE/DOCTOR: over seventy
LITTLE GIRL: seven or eight
PAULA: forties

The double casting in *Red Lips* is intentional.

Setting

The parts of the play that don't occur "at home" take place in any green country that is, in places, not so green. If this is Ireland, it is an Ireland of the imagination; therefore True and Norma and the Waiter may or may not sound Irish, but if they do, they should use stage accents rather than authentic.

Production History

Red Lips premiered at Alberta Theatre Projects, Calgary, in February, 2001, with the following cast:

CHARLIE/STATUE	Dennis Fitzgerald
JANIE	Maggie Nagle
SARAH/NORMA	Laura Parken
MYRTLE/DOCTOR/OLD WOMAN	Valerie Ann Pearson
KY/TRUE	Val Planche
PAULA	Stephanie Wolfe
GUARD/WAITER	Saxon DeCocq
LITTLE GIRL	Hannah Stickland

Directed by Paula Danckert
Composer/Sound Design by Kevin McGugan
Costume Design by David Boechler
Lighting Design by Brian Pincott
Set and Properties Design by Scott Reid
Festival Dramaturg: Bob White
Production Stage Manager: Dianne Goodman
Stage Manager: Lisa Roy Munro
Assistant Stage Manager: Crystal Fitzgerald Beatty

Notes on the Text

Dashes indicate a character's thought interrupted by herself. There is no point in the play at which characters interrupt one another.

Ellipses indicate a character's thought trailing off, becoming silent. Therefore, the thought should not be completed aloud.

Where characters' speeches are written in paragraphs, the breaks are half-pauses, time for thinking those half-thoughts that are part of an interior dialogue.

Pauses are part of the meaning as well as the rhythm of the dialogue.

"Fuckin" is used by the characters more for rhythm than emphasis.

Act One

Scene One

> *A city sidewalk in the rain. JANIE, SARAH and KY are bustling along with their umbrellas up.*

JANIE: This country is wonderful.

> *Pause.*

SARAH: Oh yes it's wonderful.

KY: Oh yes wonderful.

JANIE: So different from home.

SARAH: So different, yes.

JANIE: Green.

SARAH: It's as green as they say it is.

KY: There's no getting away from green.

> *Pause.*

JANIE: These people know how to have fun.

SARAH: They do.

KY: They sure do.

JANIE: We're having a great time.

SARAH: A great time.

KY: Great.

JANIE: We are.

SARAH: Aren't we?

KY: Oh sure we are.

Scene Two

In the lobby of a national museum. A GUARD is standing on the sidelines.

JANIE: We're here. Let's go in.

KY: Museums are boring. And my feet hurt.

SARAH: Mine too. I'm tired of being a tourist.

JANIE: If you can think of anything better to do.

KY: Swim in the ocean, loll on a beach?

SARAH: It's raining, Ky.

KY: Drink ourselves pie-eyed? Something in the present moment? *(In a low voice, indicating the guard who is looking at them.)* Hey, Janie, look—

SARAH: We could go to the art gallery.

KY: No. We'd only get wet trying to find the art gallery and anyway, it's a fact that you can only see one piece of art in a day.

JANIE: Apprehend. Look at what?

KY: *Apprehend? (Whispering.)* That guard. He's watching you.

JANIE: He is not. You can only *apprehend* one piece of art in a day. You could see considerably more.

KY: Oh for pity's sake.

JANIE: Sorry. I expect the same goes for museums. One arti*fact* per day.

KY: You're an artifact.

SARAH: She means you're turning into an old lady, Janie.

JANIE: Some day I'll be a lovely old lady.

KY: *(Low.)* I'd say that man's definitely interested.

> *The GUARD and JANIE look at one another across the room, a momentary mutual attraction.*

JANIE: *(Low.)* We're going home tomorrow. I'm not about to pick up a museum guard.

SARAH: You're the only person I know who looks forward to growing old.

JANIE: I do look forward to growing old. I'll wear pearls and sweater sets, I'll wear my trouser bottoms rolled. I'll be like the old ladies on the bus tours, taking notes of everything the tour guide says. I'll flutter my hand in the air and call out in my old lady voice: "Excuse me, but did Cromwell sleep here, did you say?" And scribble it down if he did.

SARAH: Will you remember you made fun of them when you were young?

JANIE: That will be one of the many things I'll forget.

KY: It costs money to get in here. Is it worth it if we can only *apprehend* one thing?

JANIE: It is. If you're receptive and one thing—one *artifact*—lodges in your brain, it'll stay with you. You'll take it home. It'll be yours.

KY: Janie...

SARAH: Okay, I've got an idea. To kill the time till dinner.

KY: It's only four now Sarah.

SARAH: Till we can decently go for a drink.

KY: Now she's talking.

SARAH: We'll go inside and separate and each of us will find one thing, like Janie says, then we'll meet outside—say in half an hour?

KY: And compare notes?

SARAH: Yes.

JANIE: You can't stride in there and expect to find what's yours; you can't know in advance what it is. It has to find you.

KY: My advice is to be as unreceptive as possible. Barge in there with a chip on your shoulder. Unearned rewards are sweetest.

JANIE: But that's what I'm saying. It's when it's hot and overcrowded and people have been knocking into you and you're only looking for an exit—then your thing—calls you. You recognize—

SARAH: *(Teasing.)* Its voice?

JANIE: Well. You know what I mean.

It might not seem like anything important now.

More a whisper than a voice.

But if it's your thing, it'll sneak in between the folds of that tripy brain of yours. It'll bed down there maybe for years and years. You'll go home and you'll forget about it, then someday it will surface—like a photograph that slips out of a book.

> *JANIE watches as an OLD WOMAN approaches the GUARD and asks him a question. He points out a direction to her.*

A photograph you forgot you ever took.

KY: Okay. Let's go in.

Scene Three

A room in the museum.

KY is standing in front of a glass cube.

JANIE enters.

JANIE: There you are Ky. Where's Sarah?

KY: She went to see the Vikings. Apparently her ancestors are Vikings. Or were.

JANIE: Oh.

KY: First I heard of it, too.

JANIE: Can't you picture her, though, at the bow of a ship, with her hair sailing out behind her.

KY: And sheep's horns on her head. Sheep's horns? Is that what they wore? I'm staying right here. My feet are starting to whine. Audibly. This is going to be my thing.

The GUARD enters.

JANIE: *(Noticing the GUARD.)* What a lot of gold.

KY: It's a gold exhibit. Gold throughout the ages.

JANIE: What are these?

KY: Gold balls.

JANIE: They look like a giant's necklace. Two, four, six—nine gold balls. Like big beads.

KY: Hammered gold.

JANIE: And each one seamed, do you see Ky? Most of them look a little defeated, don't they? A bit battered. It makes them kind of endearing.

KY: My feet hurt. I'm going to stand here until these balls speak to me.

The GUARD exits.

JANIE: *(Bending to read the card on the cube.)* "These hollow gold balls were of later Bronze Age, found at Tumna Cross in 1834. Eleven balls were found when a group of men were tilling land near Tumna Cross church. The balls were divided among the men, who sold them to various collectors. Gradually, over 150 years, nine balls were acquired by the Royal Academy and the National Museum. One is owned by the Archeology and Antiquities Museum. The other's whereabouts remain unknown."

KY: Whereabouts? Can one ball have whereabouts?

JANIE: That's not the point. The point is...somewhere...

KY: There's a missing ball.

JANIE: The eleventh ball... Ky, think about it...

KY: Uh-huh.

SARAH enters.

(To SARAH.) How were the Vikings?

Sarah?

SARAH is staring at the exhibit, enthralled.

Sarah?

Several moments of suspension, nothing happens. The women stand motionless, focussing on the contents of the cube.

The OLD WOMAN hobbles on. Only JANIE sees her. The OLD WOMAN reaches into the glass cube and picks up the gold balls, which now are strung like beads in a huge necklace. JANIE thinks the necklace is for her, and steps forward, but the OLD WOMAN lifts it and holds it out for SARAH's

> neck. *A bright golden light shines down on SARAH's head. SARAH walks out of the room as if no one in it exists. The gold light fades. The OLD WOMAN replaces the beads and exits.*

KY: Janie? Janie?

JANIE: What?

KY: Could we go now?

JANIE: What?

KY: Sarah's gone out to the lobby.

JANIE: Just a minute. I want to write this down.

> *JANIE gets out a pen and starts to write the information from the card on the back of an envelope.*

What? What are you laughing at?

KY: You. Go ahead, write it down. But remember, you're the one who made fun of the old ladies taking notes.

JANIE: At least I'm some use in the world. If only to be mocked.

KY: Better buy that sweater set, it's coming sooner than you think.

Scene Four

> *Lobby.*
>
> *The GUARD holds the door open for SARAH.*

KY: Look at Sarah. She's licking the cream from her chops. Must be the male attention.

JANIE: I don't suppose the guards here hold the door open for most of the visitors.

KY: No.

JANIE: *(Whispering.)* And he was supposed to be interested in me.

KY: Sorry.

JANIE: Don't be silly.

> *The GUARD watches JANIE as she follows Sarah through the door.*

JANIE: *(Noticing the GUARD.)* What is it Sarah?

SARAH: *(Whispering, excited and happy.)* I have it.

KY: What?

SARAH: I have it. In my top dresser drawer at home. The missing gold ball. It seems incredible, doesn't it? But after all, someone has to have it.

KY: Just like someone has to win the lottery. *(Aside to JANIE.)* And wouldn't you know it would be Sarah?

> *They put up their umbrellas and stroll off.*

Scene Five

> *On KY's back deck.*

JANIE: There's always a let-down, when you come home from a trip. You're tired, for one thing.

KY: It's not that.

JANIE: And Sarah's not the only one who has it all. You do too. You have a husband, a family. Your kids have turned out great. They're living their lives... Your work's going well...

KY: Oh yeah. You know, I was thinking. I don't like myself.

JANIE:	Oh Ky.
KY:	Oh Janie. Why can't I be honest?
JANIE:	It's post-trip depression.
KY:	No. I was looking out my window in the night and I had this—insight. The garden is mine. I do all the work in it. And it's fine that I own it, or think I do. But the house… The house I share with Brian, but it has my feel. I've arranged all the furniture, I pick up and put away his mess. I was thinking: I wonder how it is to live in a house completely arranged by someone else. Maybe things, their placement, the ownership of them, matters less to him than to me. But if not—then I've usurped the house. And all our possessions. God, what does that say about me? Monster materialist? Manipulator?

How can she have that ball—all this time sitting in her dresser drawer? I mean, I picked those gold balls. They were *my* thing.

Did you hear what I just said? |
| JANIE: | Oh yes. I heard what you said. |

Scene Six

In a park.

JANIE is sitting on a swing. She is swinging a little. A LITTLE GIRL enters.

LITTLE GIRL:	You're too old to cry.
JANIE:	I'm not crying.
LITTLE GIRL:	You're too old to swing too.
JANIE:	What's your name?

LITTLE GIRL: Janie.

JANIE: That's my name.

> *JANIE gets off the swing and walks away. The LITTLE GIRL follows her. They stop in front of a window.*

LITTLE GIRL: We're here.

JANIE: Where?

LITTLE GIRL: It's a jewellery store. See all the jewellery in the window?

> *They stand for a few moments, unmoving.*

I want that ruby ring. Will you buy it for me?

JANIE: *(Coldly.)* No.

LITTLE GIRL: You could buy it for me. You have enough money.

JANIE: Go away.

> *The LITTLE GIRL exits.*
>
> *JANIE enters the jewellery store. A bell tinkles and CHARLIE appears behind the counter.*

CHARLIE: Can I help you?

JANIE: I'd like to see—some rings.

CHARLIE: Rings? Any particular rings?

JANIE: No. No. You look familiar.

CHARLIE: Like someone you met before?

JANIE: Like someone I didn't meet.

> *Smiling, CHARLIE brings out a tray of rings and she takes one then another, holds them up.*

CHARLIE: *(Watching her.)* What do you think of this?

JANIE: No, I don't think so.

CHARLIE: How about this one?

JANIE: Well... I don't know.

CHARLIE: This one?

JANIE: No. Don't you have more? In the window? I thought I saw some in the window.

CHARLIE: In the window.

He gets the ruby ring.

This ruby ring was in the window. Did you mean this ruby ring?

JANIE: That must have been the one I saw.

Pause.

Can I try it on?

He hands it to her. Something distracts him.

CHARLIE: Excuse me.

While CHARLIE is distracted, JANIE puts the ring on her finger and holds her hand up to look at it.

Pause.

She puts her hand down.

JANIE: Oh, I can't make up my mind today—I'll come back tomorrow.

CHARLIE: Fine.

JANIE walks out with the ring on her finger. A red light glows just ahead of her. She steps beneath it and stands grinning. The light dies.

JANIE: *(Horrified.)* What have I done?

Scene Seven

The jewellery store. The next day.

JANIE enters, a bell tinkles and CHARLIE appears behind the counter.

JANIE: Hi. I came back.

CHARLIE: I see.

JANIE: Could I see the rings again?

CHARLIE: Certainly.

Pause.

JANIE: I can't remember which ones I looked at, really. Or which ones I liked. There were so many... I got confused.

CHARLIE: Confused.

JANIE: Well... there were...

CHARLIE: So many.

JANIE: Yes.

CHARLIE: I thought you preferred the ruby ring.

JANIE: Oh.

CHARLIE: Yes, I'm sure it was the ruby ring you admired most. I remember how you slid it onto your finger and held your hand up to the light. Something about the precious stones makes people feel like they're in church. That was the look on your face when you held it to the light. You might have been looking at a stained glass window. The Crucifixion of Christ. Or in the days before Christ, you might have been standing in your bower, at your window of blue glass. Or in the days before bowers, you might have been standing at sunset on a cliff, on the land furthest west, watching the brightness and glory of the sun on the sea.

I'll get the ruby ring for you. That way, you won't become confused, at having too much choice.

Now let me see.

Several moments go by while he pretends to look for the ring.

JANIE: Could I see that one?

CHARLIE: Yesterday you didn't give it a second look.

JANIE: But today—

CHARLIE: Have you changed so much overnight? I know it's the prevailing wisdom, that a person isn't the same individual she was even a minute before, but I've noticed a remarkable similarity in the people I've known to their previous selves. Yes, if anything, people seem to get more themselves as they get older. Do you find that happening to you?

JANIE: I don't know.

CHARLIE: You've thought about growing older?

JANIE: Yes. Yes I have.

CHARLIE: I can't seem to find the ruby ring. Do you know what I think? As I look through these rings? Unable to put my finger on the ruby ring?

I think you think that's a rhetorical question. But it's not. No it's not rhetorical at all. It's a real, live question. Would you care to tender a real, live answer? Tell me what I think.

JANIE starts to back away. In a flash, he's out from the counter and has her by the arm.

No, no. Not yet. You're going to tell me what I

think. Because I know you've read my mind. Now. I mean it.

JANIE: You think I stole the ring.

CHARLIE: I do.

JANIE: I did. I came back to return it. Honestly, that's why I'm here. I don't know what –

CHARLIE: Got into you?

JANIE: Yes.

CHARLIE: Maybe it's your natural criminal tendency?

How many times in your life has it got into you to steal a ring?

JANIE: Never.

CHARLIE: 'Never' is a big word. You could make a good argument that never is the biggest word in the English language. When I was younger, I thought the biggest word was 'forever,' but I was seeing through a glass darkly. Or I was on a ship sailing through black clouds to a western shore, and my history hadn't happened yet.

He lets go of her arm and returns behind the counter.

JANIE: I came to return it.

CHARLIE: Thought you'd slip it back into the tray among the other rings? When I wasn't looking? When some other customers came in and distracted me? Did you really think I didn't see you steal it in the first place?

JANIE: You saw me?

CHARLIE: I saw you. I read your eyes. And then I followed you home. Yes. That's a valuable ring. I simply said to those other customers, "You'll have to excuse me, I'm closing the store now. That woman just stole a ring." They scuttled right out.

I know where you live, Janie. I know where you work. I know who you are. I'm quite a detective. And I understand you. You know why? Because every once in a while something gets into me. It's called desire. Same as gets into you.

JANIE: Here. Take it. Take it back. Call the police. Whatever.

CHARLIE: Whatever. Cute. Janie, here's the deal. Dinner at a restaurant, and something precious, yes, something precious from you. Say, sex at your place. Yes, dinner at a restaurant, sex at your place, we forget it happened. Or I really do call the police.

Your apartment, at seven.

Scene Eight

In a restaurant. JANIE, SARAH and KY are sitting at a table.

SARAH: I love going for lunch. We should do it once a week. And I really need your advice. What am I going to do with that gold ball? I mean, do I have a moral obligation to hand it over to their government?

Neither of the others answers.

Excuse me? I'm serious. I love the thing. My grandmother gave it to me. But, after all, it just sits in my dresser drawer. And...

KY: You should do what—you feel like doing.

SARAH: I feel like keeping it. Especially now. It's like—I own a secret. And my grandmother told me to keep it, she said I was to give it to my eldest grand-daughter. You know, none of my family was ever wealthy or important. My grandparents and parents didn't leave an inheritance… Only this one thing. Like a fairy tale. And I always thought of it that way; it was the thing that made me special. I never even told you about it Ky.

KY: But you're not exactly Cinderella either.

Sorry.

SARAH: No. It's okay. I'm boring you.

KY: No you're not. Janie, could you say something?

JANIE: What?

KY: For pity's sake, take part in the conversation.

SARAH: Ky? What's wrong?

KY: Nothing. I'm not myself. I don't know who I am. Nobody loves me. Christ. That's exactly how I feel.

SARAH: Brian loves you. Your kids love you.

KY: Fuck. I know that. I'm in such a bad mood. It must be menopause.

SARAH: You're not old enough for menopause.

KY: You have to say that to be kind.

I just need to get back into routine. Or maybe I'm depressed at the idea of getting back into routine. I feel as if I've lost something…but I don't know what.

Pause.

JANIE: How often do you guys have sex?

And how many guys have you had sex with?

Scene Nine

Evening. In front of JANIE's apartment building.

JANIE is pacing up and down. CHARLIE enters.

CHARLIE: Hey—lookin' good!

JANIE: What?

CHARLIE: You are looking great!

I mean it. Superb! Superior! All of that stuff!

My God you've got legs! You've got it all!

And you flaunt it! I love that in a woman! I love it!

Fuck! This is gonna be one great night! On the town! That's us! Baby.

JANIE: Look—I don't even know your name.

CHARLIE: Call me Irresistible.

JANIE: Look I can't—I really can't—

CHARLIE: I mean it baby—there is no stopping me. You hear now? Hot time in the old town tonight. This is it. What you've always wanted.

Look at you. Red fingernails. Red lips, in this grey world.

JANIE: Listen—

CHARLIE: Know what your problem is? Of course you know what your problem is. It's me. Yes? Baby? No—say nothing. Forget it. Look. You and me. On the town. Dinner. Sex. Hey, and you can keep the ring.

JANIE: I gave it back.

CHARLIE: Dinner awaits.

JANIE: Please...

CHARLIE: Janie. This is it.

JANIE: What?

CHARLIE: This is it. This is all there is.

JANIE: No.

CHARLIE: Oh yes.

Scene Ten

A restaurant. Subdued, expensive atmosphere. Muted saxophone playing.

JANIE: I don't want champagne.

CHARLIE: Tea? You want tea?

JANIE: Tea! No.

CHARLIE: Well then have champagne. I'm ordering a bottle. Why not?

JANIE: I'm only here to talk. I want to tell you— It's your word against mine.

CHARLIE: No.

JANIE: What?

CHARLIE: You forget the world you live in. Sorry, but— Video surveillance, my dear Janie. Has captured you, with your grubby little fingers in the rings. With your hand out, like this, admiring that ruby. Its stained glass light. And just a few moments later, with the ruby turned down, towards your palm, just before you clenched your fist and shoved it into your pocket and left the store. Just after you said to me: I can't make up my mind. It's all there: you in living colour. And the colour is red.

JANIE: Who are you? What's your name?

CHARLIE: Mr. Allnut.

JANIE: Mr. Allnut? You want me to call you Mr. Allnut?

CHARLIE: I do.

JANIE: God. Listen. I'll sit here with you. We'll talk. We're not having sex. I'm not doing that.

CHARLIE: I'm not doing that, Mr. Allnut.

JANIE: What?

CHARLIE: Just trying to get you into the rhythm of the evening.

JANIE: You are a nut all right. God, truer words were never— Mr. All-nut.

CHARLIE: Don't laugh.

JANIE: Then don't be stupid.

CHARLIE: Do you think I'm stupid? And vulgar? And beneath you? You'd never go out with the likes of me, eh? If I asked you on a date? Would you? Would you?

JANIE: How can I know that? You didn't. This is blackmail.

CHARLIE: I don't see it that way. I'm giving you a chance, that's all. You're trapped. It's a way out. Think of this dinner as a boat, floating you down a river, away from a place of danger. To a new adventure.

JANIE: I would never go anywhere with you. You're despicable.

CHARLIE: You're a common thief.

JANIE: You're taking advantage. Treating me like an object.

CHARLIE: Oh ho. You're willing.

JANIE: What?

CHARLIE: To barter. To use your body, yourself. Hey, it's one night. How bad can it be?

JANIE: I'd rather go to jail.

CHARLIE: It's not jail you're worried about. Janie my dear. Maybe you'd get a suspended sentence. Though that's one expensive ring. That matters, you know. It costs more if it costs more. No, what you're worried about is the gossip. Mmm? You're alone, at what? Forty. So what's the problem? Repressed old maid? That's it, right? Repressed old maid steals a ruby ring. I don't know, but it seems to me your friends could talk about this for months…

You should be grateful to me. I'm trying to do you a favour.

Scene Eleven

At KY's place.

SARAH: I've lost it.

KY: How?

SARAH: I don't know. I can't find it. It's not in my dresser drawer. The box is there, the box I keep it in, but the ball's gone. It must have been stolen.

KY: Stolen? Who would have stolen it? Was your house broken into? Was anything else taken?

SARAH: No. Nothing else was taken.

KY: Then it can't have been stolen. Who would have known you had it…? Maybe one of your kids took it? To play with. Or to show their friends. Sarah, that must be it.

SARAH: I asked them. I thought of that.

KY:	Maybe they wouldn't want to admit it. They'd feel ashamed... I'll bet you'll find it back in its box when you get home.
SARAH:	My kids wouldn't lie to me.
KY:	Who else knows about it? Because if your house wasn't broken into, and if nothing else was taken... Janie and I, your kids...
SARAH:	No.
KY:	Well I didn't take it. And I don't imagine Janie... Sarah? When Janie dropped you off after lunch, did she go in?
SARAH:	Just to pick up a book she'd lent— Oh Ky, it's too silly.

Scene Twelve

In the restaurant.

JANIE and CHARLIE are drinking champagne.

CHARLIE:	Down the river. We go. Down the river to the sea. It's you who's taking us Janie. On this journey. Here's to you. A woman of spunk and courage.
JANIE:	I am not a woman of spunk.
CHARLIE:	You're taking me on. Yes you are. You don't give up easily. You're a fighter, Janie.
JANIE:	I'm an idiot.
	She stands up.
CHARLIE:	Where are you going?
JANIE:	To the washroom. Do you mind?
CHARLIE:	You're beautiful when you're angry.

"To the washroom. Do you mind? Mr. Allnut?" I'm sorry Miss, but I do like that fire in your eyes.

JANIE walks away. CHARLIE tops up their glasses.

In the washroom, JANIE at the mirror.

JANIE: God my face is red.

I am an idiot. He's a psychopath.

(Mocking, exasperated with herself.) "You're beautiful when you're angry."

JANIE returns to the table.

CHARLIE: Let's have the lobster.

JANIE: Have what you want.

CHARLIE: Thanks. What's your favourite movie?

JANIE: I don't know.

CHARLIE: Mine's *The African Queen*.

JANIE: *(Catching on to the name.)* Mr. Allnut.

CHARLIE: That's right.

JANIE: God.

CHARLIE: So you've seen it. You see what I mean, about going down the river. I think it will help you to look on this as an adventure.

JANIE: Katharine Hepburn and Humphrey Bogart.

CHARLIE: Rosie Whatsername, and Charlie Allnut. We do have something in common with them. They're a little…on the mature side, for romance. And then, they got off on the wrong foot too.

JANIE: Got off on the wrong foot!

CHARLIE: You can tell, at the beginning of the movie, she thinks she's too good for him. And I'll tell you a secret. He thinks so too.

JANIE: We are nothing like them.

CHARLIE: Your face gets red. And you're all stiff and formal, like she is. Until she learns to love him.

Pause.

You're awfully quiet. You're thinking, aren't you? How can I get away? Could I walk out of here and take an airplane somewhere and never go back to my apartment, and would that work? Would that keep me from ever seeing him again? You think I'm sick.

JANIE: You are sick.

CHARLIE: Maybe I love you.

JANIE: You don't know me.

CHARLIE: Nobody knows you. Don't you think that's a tragedy?

Pause.

JANIE: Look. I have something for you. I brought you something. I want to give it to you.

CHARLIE: Something you stole?

JANIE: No.

She takes the gold ball from her bag and sets it on the table between them.

It's gold. My grandmother gave it to me, when I was a little girl. I want you to have it. It's special, you see. It's the missing piece of a set. You could solve the mystery, if you want. I think it would be fun, don't you? And they'd pay quite well for it… Don't laugh.

CHARLIE: You're not very bright, are you? You think I'd want this thing? Poor old beaten up thing. You can't give this to me. I don't want it. That wasn't the deal. You remember the deal.

Pause.

Do you remember that scene, early on in the movie, when Charlie's having tea with Rosie and her brother—and his stomach rumbles?

JANIE: No.

CHARLIE: It's a scene you can't believe in. The sound—it's supposed to be his stomach—it gurgles and growls and he gawks around and grins like an idiot while the others pretend they don't hear it.

It's so over the top, if Hepburn and Bogart were different people you'd give up on it right there. It's Hepburn and Bogart who keep you watching. The characters are stupid—caricatures—but you can see real people behind them. Their intelligent eyes. Promising you something real.

That's where we are.

JANIE: I don't know what you mean.

CHARLIE: We have a chance to get real. I know you don't believe it. Listen. When you came into the store, I saw: educated, professional, nice. A nice woman. That's the role you were playing. Your eyes said something else.

JANIE: My eyes—

CHARLIE: Were hungry. Even primitive.

JANIE: Oh really—

CHARLIE: Charlie Allnut's stomach rumbling was like that—revealing him as a primal being, without that crackling veneer that Rosie wore. You were more

	subtle. Your eyes, and your—aura, or whatever it is you emanate—excitement—the air around you trembled. When you looked at those rings. I knew you were going to steal something. I wanted you to do it.
JANIE:	You're romanticizing what is in fact banal. I *am* a common thief.
	I stole this from my friend.
CHARLIE:	Let's start over. Clean.
JANIE:	No—
CHARLIE:	We can if we want to.
JANIE:	We're strangers.
CHARLIE:	Let's be better strangers.
JANIE:	I wish we could be complete strangers. It would be the best thing we could be.
	You forced me to come out with you.
CHARLIE:	You wouldn't have come if I'd just asked you.
JANIE:	You don't know that.
CHARLIE:	Would you have?
JANIE:	If your eyes had been kind…
CHARLIE:	Don't cry.
JANIE:	I'm not crying. I'm ashamed. To behave the way I have, then ask for kindness… Why did you say dinner and sex? Why did you have to say that?
CHARLIE:	It was your eyes. I thought you'd enjoy the element of danger.
JANIE:	No.
CHARLIE:	I fucked up. Forget sex. I'm not a rapist. Forget it.

And I'm not going to turn you in. So, what are our possibilities?

Pause.

JANIE: I don't think there are any possibilities. In this situation.

CHARLIE: Sure there are. You could eat your lobster and then go. And while you're having dinner, you could wear this.

He hands her the ruby ring. JANIE looks up to see PAULA standing outside the restaurant, looking in the window. Charlie cannot see her.

JANIE: No.

CHARLIE: Go ahead. Just for tonight. Look at it.

JANIE: Why would I steal it? It's nothing.

CHARLIE: Nice colour. Put it on.

JANIE: What's your name?

CHARLIE: Rosie asks that. It's after they've declared their love, after they've acknowledged their feelings for one another, that's probably more accurate—she says: "What's your first name? Mr. Allnut? Dear?"

It's Charlie. Really.

JANIE: Well Charlie, I don't want to put the ring on. I'm ashamed of myself.

CHARLIE: I know. Look. No strings attached. But if we just have dinner… Sit here and talk… And we promise we'll never see each other again… Maybe we could have an hour or two where the two of us can be our real selves. Where you don't have to be that nice woman. Fuck, of course you're a nice woman. Anyone can tell by looking at you—but you're also a woman who wanted a ruby ring enough to steal

	it. A woman whose eyes were hungry— And I'm a guy who wanted *you* enough to make a despicable bargain. And if we could be those two people, those two real people—this once in your life someone would know you.
JANIE:	I'm not sure I want anyone to know me. Maybe people should protect themselves.
CHARLIE:	And stay lonely?

PAULA turns and walks off. JANIE watches her go.

JANIE slips the ring on her finger.

JANIE:	It's only a ring. I know it's worth a lot of money, but it might as well be glass.
CHARLIE:	No, it's a ruby. Knowing that it's a ruby makes all the difference.
JANIE:	Maybe. I've never stolen anything before and now two things.
CHARLIE:	Imagine stealing all the time. Every day of your life. Don't shake your head. Imagine being a thief. Quitting your job. Stealing for a living. Owning beautiful things. Expensive things. Imagine wearing jewels. Possessing all you want. Everything you want.
JANIE:	That's not what I want. I want to be good, and I'm not. I want to do good, and I don't.
CHARLIE:	Bullshit. You want gold and rubies. You want what they mean to you. Adventure. You don't have all the time in the world, Janie. For the things you want. Energy. Power. Sex. Do you want sex, Janie?
JANIE:	I do want it. And want for it. I wish for it. If I prayed, I'd pray for it. But it makes a woman vulnerable.
CHARLIE:	Don't you think it does the same for a man?

JANIE: Does it?

CHARLIE: To be honest, I don't think it does.

JANIE: Who are you?

CHARLIE: You know who I am. I'm the one who looks into your eyes.

JANIE: My eyes—

CHARLIE: Are hungry. Primitive.

JANIE: Oh really—

CHARLIE: Fuck-me eyes. Like I said before, I'm at your service.

> *Pause.*
>
> *JANIE turns away from CHARLIE.*

JANIE: *(Surprised.)* When I turn away from you I hear the ocean.

CHARLIE: We're a thousand miles from any ocean.

JANIE: But I hear it. Pounding on the cliffs. Boom.

CHARLIE: It's elemental, my dear Watson.

JANIE: And I hear your words.

And if I stand up...

> *She stands.*

And walk away...

> *She takes a few steps and stops.*

I hear a river. Water bubbling over rock. And— whiz! The fisherman testing his reel.

> *Her head jerks back as if she has been hooked.*

And I hear your words.

What you said about my lifting my hand to look at the ruby ring. You said the precious stones make people feel like they're in church. You said that was the look on my face when I held it to the light. You said I might have been looking at a stained glass window. The Crucifixion of Christ. Or in the days before Christ, I might have been standing in my bower, at my window of blue glass. Or in the days before bowers, I might have been standing at sunset on a cliff, on the land furthest west, watching the brightness and glory of the sun on the sea.

And what you said when I used the word 'never.' That when you were younger, you thought the biggest word was 'forever,' but you were seeing through a glass darkly. Or you were on a ship sailing through black clouds to a western shore, and your history hadn't happened yet.

Pause.

And what you said when you met me outside my apartment: Red lips, in this grey world.

She returns to her chair, pulls it out, sits.

This is it. What I've always wanted. Always— wanted.

Scene Thirteen

In an airport lounge.

JANIE is sitting on the edge of her seat.

An old woman, ROSE, enters carrying a notebook. For a moment she observes JANIE. Then she sits beside her.

ROSE: Have you been waiting long?

JANIE: We're on standby. We'll be on this next plane.

ROSE: Time passes so quickly in your middle years.

JANIE: I guess it does. Except in airports.

ROSE: Weeks and months go by, so filled with work, with projects and details, you think: how can it be March already?

JANIE: Yes.

ROSE: I remember my mother saying to me on the telephone once: you will have a busy February. She said it quite matter-of-factly, but it came to me that I had had a busy Christmas season and January was hectic, and I had not visited her as often as I meant to, certainly not as often as she would have liked.

Time is different for the old. The years whip by, a whole year can pass like the pages of a calendar in an old movie, but the hours seem long.

I had a very nice holiday last summer. On a bus tour. And I made notes. It's a good idea to do that. Photographs can make you sad. I went on the tour with my husband. We had been married and he had been my dear friend for fifty years. He died recently. That's the other thing that happens while time is being perverse. Your friends are dying. It's no good pretending otherwise.

But my notes. Yes, I have no idea why I wrote some of them. They are only scraps. Sentences come into my head, especially when I'm away from home, in a strange land.

JANIE: You take notes?

ROSE: I wrote the first one when we were on a little island. Where we found a huge empty beach. I wrote: "The surf has molded striations up the dunes; they might be modelled on the veins on the backs of my hands."

You wonder: does time—is time molding us? And are we as shiftless as the dunes? Or do I mean as shiftable? As easily shifted as sand in the dunes.

Another bit was: "While the moon rose we leaned over the Mulvey and watched a fisherman test his reel." I don't know what you'll make of that.

We were walking home after dinner, crossing the little bridge; the river in the evening light was silvered and rippled, so that the water looked like fish scales or chain mail, almost unmoving between the lush banks and tall green trees; it was as picturesque as a jigsaw puzzle picture, and it seemed as if time had stopped when we stopped, and the only thing alive was the man fishing.

I suppose in a way, it's opposite to the first thing I wrote. It's active instead of passive. About testing, trying. Trying to catch something.

It was the most beautiful evening.

Finally CHARLIE arrives, looks at JANIE from across the room, and JANIE rises and goes to him.

Scene Fourteen

KY and SARAH enter in their own space.

KY: What in the world's going on?

SARAH: I don't know. I don't know.

KY: Did she give you any explanation?

SARAH: Oh no. She just came to the house with her face all glowing and said she didn't know what had got into her. She took the ball out of her shoulder bag and handed it over.

KY: And she's gone away? With this man she's known two days?

SARAH: She's gone. I don't know where. I don't know why.

KY: That's all she said? I'm going away... off somewhere with... What's his name?

SARAH: Charlie. That's the only name she gave me.

KY: The adorable, unknown Charlie.

SARAH: Mmm-hmm. Oh, and she said: he wants to know me. When I asked why she was doing this, she said: he wants to know me.

KY: I'd feel a lot better if she knew him.

Scene Fifteen

On a cliff overlooking the ocean.

JANIE: I never knew, I never thought, I never believed I could live like this. Why did you bring me here?

CHARLIE: To see you here.

JANIE: I feel—

It's so wild and beautiful. With this mist. Ghostly. As if we're moving, the cliff and you and I, out, drifting out... And all the people who have stood here looking west, all through history, are with us, moving out...toward the sea.

Is this the land furthest west?

I can't believe we're going to live here. We're going to live in this strange stone cottage. With its round windows like two eyes.

CHARLIE: The better to look out to sea.

He holds his hands out to her.

JANIE: What big hands you have, grandmother...

Scene Sixteen

KY and SARAH's space.

SARAH: I did it. Sent it off.

KY: Good for you.

SARAH: I hope so. Anyway, I don't have a daughter to pass it down to.

KY: I thought it would have gone to your granddaughter.

SARAH: Yes, it was supposed to. Since my grandmother gave it to me. Oh well, it belongs there. It's part of their past, not ours. And I feel relieved.

There was something wrong about it, about owning it, once I knew. Why would I want to keep a thing that wasn't mine? I felt uneasy. Yes, uneasy. With it in the house. I wanted it gone.

Scene Seventeen

At the cottage windows.

Sound of wind, distant angry ocean.

JANIE: You have your window; I have mine. What do you see, Charlie? From your window?

CHARLIE: No doubt I see what you see.

JANIE: On the way home today I saw a woman on the cliffs. She was watching the cottage.

When I look out, I seem to see her still.

Do you see her?

CHARLIE: No.

JANIE: What do you see?

CHARLIE:	I see you. With wind in your hair and salt water stinging your face. That would not be sea spray but your own tears.
JANIE:	But I'm quite happy.

Scene Eighteen

KY and SARAH's space.

KY:	I can't believe it.
SARAH:	After all that fuss.
KY:	All the worry.
SARAH:	Trying to do the right thing.
KY:	You did the right thing.
SARAH:	It isn't even the right effing ball. It isn't even gold.
KY:	It looked gold to me.
SARAH:	It's a sleigh bell. That's what they say in the letter. Oh Ky, it sounds so snooty. "We believe the object you sent, Madam, is commonly known as a sleigh bell. Commonly attached to a horse's harness. As it may have sentimental value, we return it post-haste." It's a brass ball! Well the joke's on me.
KY:	No, the joke's on us all.
SARAH:	Fool's gold, that's what it was. God Ky, they must have laughed when they saw it, those people at the museum.
KY:	Those museum types need a good laugh.
SARAH:	I told them all about my grandmother giving it to me, and they said,
	"Perhaps it was from a favourite horse."
KY:	Maybe it was.

SARAH:	Maybe. My kids told their teachers at school. The whole school knows about it.
KY:	Oh no.
SARAH:	Oh yes. Their mother, nobly returning a family heirloom to its rightful place.
KY:	But you did it. It's what you did. The act counts.
SARAH:	Sure. Consider me noble.
KY:	They will. Eventually.

Scene Nineteen

On the cliff. Sunny day, the ocean booming.

JANIE enters and walks toward the cottage. She is carrying a shopping basket with groceries, bread and wine.

CHARLIE comes out of the cottage.

JANIE: Charlie, I'm so happy.

I'm on high. I'm on air. There is no ground under my feet.

I could fly to you, fly with you, knock you off your feet, bowl you over, buoy you up, carry you off, wrap my arms, wrap my heart around you—

She stops when she sees PAULA, who comes out of the cottage and walks away.

Scene Twenty

At the cottage. Pre-dawn. The muffled sound of the ocean.

JANIE: Somehow the moon got into the bedroom. It was in the corner, over to the left. I woke up and there it was. You were lying beside me, wearing armour. I mean, a full suit of armour, visor and all. You were lying there snoring beside me, almost like a husband. And I could see these two points in the sheets at the foot of the bed where your feet were sticking up in those ridiculous metal shoes.

There was a silvery light in the room. We looked black and white, like an old film. And there was the moon. A huge, full, pock-marked, luminous moon, hanging in the corner of the room. I could hear the surf and with every surge, the moon swelled. It grew and grew. I sat up in bed watching. You slept on. The walls began to bulge.

I slipped out of bed and went outside, into the night. I walked away from the cottage, away from the cliffs, and I looked up and there was the moon, the ordinary every night proper little moon, high in the black sky. I was relieved to find it there, in its right place.

CHARLIE stands up and looks her in the eye. JANIE half-rises to him, and he puts his hand on the top of her head and pushes her down.

He exits.

She sits alone, suspended, listening to the ocean.

JANIE: I can't stay here.

I suppose I'll go home.

No one will have expected anything else.

The sun rises. JANIE sits, unmoving.

Act Two

Scene One

A public square. It's night and it's raining.

In the centre of the square is a STATUE of a man. It looks like CHARLIE. Two homeless women, TRUE and NORMA, are sleeping under the STATUE.

JANIE enters; she carries an umbrella. She is quite drunk. She walks around the STATUE, which has no marker to identify it.

JANIE: Well, who the hell are you anyway?

Some man. Some man who sometime did something for someone.

More likely did something to someone. Killed 'em or beat 'em down or somehow sucked the living daylights out of 'em, and thus became a success in the world.

A big man. Put your dukes up!

TRUE: Shut up, you.

JANIE: Come down off your pedestal, asshole! You think I couldn't hurt you?

NORMA: Shut your fuckin mouth, she said.

TRUE: I ask myself: True, did this drunken cow wake you? And I say: Yes she did. She did fuckin wake you True.

NORMA: She did True. You listen to yourself on that one. And I'll tell you True, me Mother used to say, if a body will wake you from your sleep, there'll be no telling what kind of fuckin rudeness she'll be up to.

TRUE: I ask myself: was she fuckin talkin to that fuckin statue?

NORMA: She was. She was fuckin askin it to fight.

TRUE: Go on then you stupid sow. Punch him a good one. Fuckin kill him would you?

JANIE: I will. I don't like his face.

I don't like his…fuckin face! He reminds me of someone. He's hiding something. I know he is. Doesn't he look smug? Impudent asshole. Cruel bastard.

TRUE: Lord, you've got to ask yourself, though: is it not the fuckin middle of the night?

NORMA: It is True. And I, Norma, must ask myself the same. Is it not the middle of the fuckin night?

JANIE climbs up to wipe the STATUE's face.

JANIE: Impervious to rain, to tears. Eyes that don't see. Lips that won't speak. And a stone cold…fuckin heart!

She kisses the STATUE on the mouth.

NORMA: Here now. Me old Mum would say he's a man after all and if there's one part left working on him it'll be between your legs before you can say skedaddle.

TRUE: A hard man is good to find.

NORMA: Me Mum said that too. I need a drink.

TRUE: Ask yourself Norma: who woke us up?

NORMA:	This one.
TRUE:	Who'd be owing us a drink then?
NORMA:	This one.
JANIE:	And it just so happens, I have here this bottle of whiskey which the bartender told me is renowned across your island.

The bottle slips from her hands and smashes on the pedestal.

TRUE & NORMA:	Oh fuck.

TRUE and NORMA exit.

JANIE:	Hey, come back! Can I come with you?

JANIE follows them off, then returns alone and sits on the pedestal. She is wide awake and afraid to be alone.

From across the square comes the low, yearning sound of a tenor saxophone. A few moments later, the sound of a window flung open.

VOICE:	Oh Jesus, will you shut up that racket! Is there no respect for sleep in this town?

The music stops.

Scene Two

KY and SARAH's space.

KY:	He's left her. She says she's staying there.

Pause.

SARAH:	What's she doing for money?
KY:	She would have had some saved.

SARAH:	Not much. The first trip took her savings.
KY:	I imagine she's using her pension fund.
SARAH:	Oh boy.
KY:	She's a big girl.
SARAH:	I guess so. Where's she staying?
KY:	She didn't say. I did ask.
SARAH:	That's odd, isn't it?
KY:	She likely needs some time alone.
SARAH:	Likely. Maybe it's for the best. It's been a while, though.
KY:	She can get another job. When she comes home.
SARAH:	That's right. Of course she can. She's hardly without resources.
KY:	Anyway, she's not asking us for our opinion.
SARAH:	Just because we're so good at giving it.

Scene Three

Morning in the square.

JANIE is still sitting on the pedestal, still awake.

Across the square, the WAITER comes out and stands looking at the sunrise.

JANIE goes over to the waiter.

JANIE:	Hi. Could I...? Could I get a coffee?
WAITER:	You could when I'm open.
JANIE:	Oh. Okay.

NORMA and TRUE enter.

The WAITER takes the chairs off the table and sets them upright on the pavement. He exits.

TRUE holds out her cap to JANIE. JANIE opens her wallet and gives True some money.

JANIE: Sorry. I don't have very much myself.

TRUE: That's a pretty ring you've got there.

JANIE: I forgot I had it still.

NORMA curls up under the STATUE's pedestal and goes to sleep.

The fact is, I'm nearly out of money. I don't have a place to stay. I thought I'd look for a job. I will. But I can't get it together. I can't think.

TRUE stares at JANIE then falls asleep.

JANIE falls asleep.

An old woman— MYRTLE—hobbles on and over to JANIE.

NORMA sits up, stretches, watches as MYRTLE slips her hands into JANIE's pockets, finds her wallet and takes it.

The WAITER enters with a cup of coffee.

JANIE wakes up to see the old woman teetering on the edge of the curb. She rushes to MYRTLE and takes her arm.

Surprised and alarmed, the old woman tries to get away but JANIE thinks she's falling and grabs her tighter.

JANIE: It's okay. I've got you. I'll help you. Come on.

Will you be okay now?

MYRTLE exits. JANIE notices NORMA laughing but returns to her table.

The WAITER hands her the coffee and the bill.

JANIE discovers the loss of her wallet.

Oh my God my wallet's gone. I—it's gone. No, really. It's been stolen. Just a minute I must have change.

WAITER: No, you're okay. It'll be on me—this morning only.

JANIE: Thank you.

WAITER: No thanks necessary.

NORMA: Hey! Hey! Sweetie! It was the old girl.

It was. Go after her. Go on with you now. Chase her.

JANIE: She took my wallet?

NORMA: While you were snoozing.

Go on. Go get it. You can run faster than that old twat can't you?

Scene Four

At the cottage on the cliffs. An overcast night. The ocean beats like a heart. The two round windows are lit with a fire's glow.

JANIE arrives. She stands looking at the cottage, suspended.

Scene Five

KY and SARAH's space.

KY: I'm on a fulcrum. At the midpoint of my life, teetering.

SARAH: But you can't go either way. I mean, there's only one direction.

KY: Oh yes it's all downhill from here.

SARAH: You could *look* back.

KY: But why? I could look forward, too, but to what? It all looks pretty foggy from here.

SARAH: But there are things to look forward to. There are things to learn. To see. To do.

KY: I would like to see a sloth. Yes, I have an affinity for the lowly sloth. In their pictures they have such doleful eyes. And they hang for hours suspended from the branches of trees, upside down, asleep. I would like to stand on my head again. I've forgotten how things look. Do things appear upside down when you're upside down? Or does your brain adjust to it and right things up? Or do you subconsciously say to yourself: I know perfectly well I'm upside down and therefore, whatever I see—

SARAH: You could easily stand on your head right now and find out. I could hold your legs.

KY: But I don't do it. No I don't do any of the things I'd vaguely like to do. I expect I'll die without ever standing on my head again. The truth is I'm too lazy to try. Think of the energy required. When I'm so cozy sitting here.

Scene Six

JANIE returns to the square in the middle of the night and sits on the STATUE's pedestal.

The sun rises. The WAITER brings JANIE a coffee.

PAULA appears, carrying a shopping basket full of groceries, bread, wine. She sees JANIE but walks on.

WAITER: Someone you know?

Pause.

JANIE: No.

The WAITER takes the chairs off the table and sets them upright.

That won't do any good you know.

She turns the table upside down.

There. Now that's a change.

Pause.

WAITER: It is, yes. You're all right, are you?

JANIE: Yes. Are you the musician?

WAITER: I'm the waiter.

JANIE: But you're the one who plays the saxophone?

WAITER: I make the racket.

JANIE: I thought it was beautiful.

WAITER: You'd be in a minority. They don't like it, here. You can't blame them. I have to practice. It's the same thing over and over. They hear it over and over. They get sick of hearing me. Anyone would.

JANIE: I wouldn't.

WAITER: The truth is, I'm not very good. The other night, I forgot myself. I don't play anymore.

Pause.

JANIE: *(Looking at the STATUE.)* Do you know who he's supposed to be?

WAITER: I don't, actually, no. Some poor bastard who thought he wouldn't be forgotten.

Does it matter?

JANIE:	No. No, I don't give a fuck who he is.
WAITER:	I can see you're the kind of woman who does not give a fuck. Yeah. I noted that immediately I set eyes on you.

Scene Seven

At the cottage on the cliffs. An overcast night. The ocean beats like a heart. The two round windows are lit with a fire's glow.

JANIE arrives. She stands looking at the cottage, suspended.

Scene Eight

Morning. JANIE is sitting in the square. TRUE is sleeping under the STATUE. NORMA is waking.

PAULA appears, carrying a shopping basket full of groceries, bread, wine. She sees JANIE but walks on.

JANIE: Wait! Please. Could I ask you something?

I'm sorry.

I couldn't let you just go by. Without...

Pause.

PAULA: Well?

JANIE: I thought I should ask you...how well you know him.

If you know what you're getting into.

Pause.

PAULA: Sweetie— Go home.

PAULA leaves.

JANIE backs up and steps on TRUE.

TRUE: Watch yourself.

JANIE: I'm sorry. I'm sorry.

NORMA: You fuckin stepped on her.

JANIE: I said I'm sorry.

TRUE: Norma, this is the second time this one's woke me up, is it not?

NORMA: Oh Jesus pity her if she makes it three.

JANIE: It was an accident and I said— Look. Couldn't we be friends?

Pause.

TRUE: What's your name?

JANIE: Janie.

TRUE: That's nice. It's nice isn't it Norma?

NORMA: Oh it's lovely. It's a lovely fuckin name.

JANIE: And you're True?

TRUE: I am. And you know what? It costs me friends. Telling the truth. For instance, if I was to ask myself, True, what advice would you give a girl not from these parts and with no talent at all for survival… Norma, what would it be?

NORMA: Me mother would say: Look into your heart.

TRUE: Your mother would not give you that shit.

Your mother would say: You don't know your own mind so I'll know it for you, and the long and the short of it is: go home.

NORMA: You heard True now Janie. There's no place for you here, whether you know it or not.

TRUE:	You're a fuckin nuisance.
NORMA:	You're not like us.
JANIE:	Why not?

Pause.

NORMA:	Your teeth would be one thing. So white and even and clean.
TRUE:	"I don't have very much myself."
JANIE:	I don't, now.
NORMA:	Ah, she lost her wallet.
JANIE:	It was stolen.
NORMA:	Myrtle.
TRUE:	Myrtle?
NORMA:	She wouldn't even chase her.
JANIE:	I don't care. I don't. What good did money ever do me?

TRUE and NORMA exchange looks.

TRUE:	If you ask me True, can money buy you love, I'd have to say no, but it's a step up to friendship. We'll be wanting to get that wallet back Norma.
NORMA:	Stand up now.
JANIE:	Stand up?
NORMA:	That's it.

JANIE stands and NORMA puts a blindfold over her eyes.

JANIE:	What?
NORMA:	We're off to locate your wallet. Myrtle won't want you to know where she lives.

TRUE and NORMA march off with JANIE between them. At times they turn her round and round and push her off balance for their enjoyment.

Come on, will you?

JANIE: I am.

NORMA: You're not.

TRUE: You're fuckin takin forever.

NORMA: Creepin along, feelin your way.

They exit. When they return, JANIE is no longer blindfolded.

JANIE: It's not my fault she wasn't home.

NORMA: She'll be out spendin your money. How much cash did you have?

JANIE: I don't know.

TRUE: Credit cards?

JANIE: A couple.

NORMA: Big party it'll be. For Myrtle alone.

Pause.

JANIE: We could have a party too.

JANIE tugs off a shoe and takes out a bill.

I still have this.

NORMA: She's a sneaky, this one.

TRUE: Smarter than she looks.

NORMA: Ask yourself, True, if she might not have another in the other shoe.

JANIE: No! It's all I have. Let's blow it. Have some fun. Let's go out tonight. The three of us.

NORMA:	You're a fuckin idiot you know.
JANIE:	I mean it. Come on.

Scene Nine

In the Revival Mission.

JANIE is holding up a sexy red dress and imagining herself in it.

JANIE:	Come on you two. I want to see you.

JANIE takes the dress to the mirror.

It's fun to get dressed up. In second-hand clothes.

You'll look fantastic.

We'll go out for dinner. We'll have a good time.

NORMA:	*(From a fitting room.)* Are you putting on that red dress?
JANIE:	I don't know… if it's me. It was easier to find dresses for you.
TRUE:	Ah fuck.
NORMA:	You put that dress on Janie. We're not coming out till you do.
TRUE:	I give up. I can't fuckin get the zipper up.
NORMA:	Stand up straight. Suck in your gut. It'll go up. Do you want help?
TRUE:	No. I do not.

There.

JANIE takes the red dress into a changing room.

I can't breathe now.

NORMA:	Take smaller breaths. Janie, are you changing yet?

JANIE: Yes.

Yes.

> *TRUE and NORMA come out, looking more like KY and SARAH than themselves. But on their feet are their old run-down shoes. They go to the mirror together, look at themselves and one another.*

TRUE: I fuckin look like someone else.

NORMA: You do True. It's like in the magazines. "Before and After." Everyone looks better before.

> *TRUE and NORMA retreat to take off their dresses.*

JANIE: Are you guys getting hungry? I'm starving.

I'm starving.

I'm going to order prawns. What are you going to have?

> *Pause.*

Norma? True?

NORMA: Oh prawns'll be good enough for the likes of us.

> *TRUE and NORMA come out in their old clothes and sneak away.*

JANIE: Or lobster... Prawns first then lobster. And champagne.

Do you guys like champagne?

> *Pause.*

> *JANIE comes out in her red dress. Seeing herself, she goes to the mirror and fluffs up her hair. She smiles at her reflection.*

True? Norma?

She looks for them in the change rooms. She sees that they've left her and looks about as if lost.

PAULA enters.

PAULA: All dressed up and no place to go?

Come.

Scene Ten

JANIE and PAULA sit at a table in a restaurant.

PAULA: I thought you seemed to want to talk.

JANIE: Oh. Yes.

Pause.

PAULA: How did you like the cottage?

Pause.

JANIE: It was fine.

PAULA: Interesting how it was designed, mmm? Those round windows like two eyes. It's a famine cottage. An entire family died there from starvation. Are you ready to order? The smoked salmon's excellent. So. What did you want to know?

You wanted to talk to me didn't you?

JANIE: Yes. Yes I think I did.

PAULA: Maybe you wanted to see what I've got that you don't have.

Maybe you wanted to...share? Sweetie. You're here. I'm here...

JANIE: I think I wanted to know—

Pause.

	If there's anything we have in common. Did he ever say you were like Katharine Hepburn in *The African Queen*?
PAULA:	Ingrid Bergman.
JANIE:	Oh.
PAULA:	*Casablanca*. So. He was—attentive? Appreciative?
JANIE:	Yes.
PAULA:	Complimentary?
JANIE:	Yes.
PAULA:	Have you met any of the others?
	Pause.
JANIE:	There were others?
PAULA:	You thought you were *special*?
	Pause.
	JANIE nods.
	Sweetie. He's already forgotten your name.
	Didn't you ever wonder why he spent so little time with you?
JANIE:	At first—
PAULA:	At first…?
JANIE:	At first he spent more time with me.
PAULA:	But then. He took everything he could get from you. Isn't that right?
	You gave and gave and gave. He *took* and *took* and *took*. And took. And soon—
JANIE:	I don't see why you're being so aggressive.

>   *PAULA opens her purse and takes out her compact and lipstick. She looks into the compact mirror and applies her lipstick carefully, absorbed in the activity.*
>
>   *JANIE reaches into the purse and takes PAULA's wallet, quickly hiding it.*

PAULA: I'm his wife. Don't be concerned. It means very little, as you should be aware.

>   *PAULA exits.*
>
>   *JANIE puts the wallet on the table, where it remains throughout the next scenes, until she returns. She exits.*

Scene Eleven

>   *At the cottage on the cliffs. An overcast night. The ocean beats like a heart. The two round windows are lit with a fire's glow.*
>
>   *JANIE arrives. She stands looking at the cottage.*
>
>   *She goes up to a window and peers inside.*

Scene Twelve

>   *KY and SARAH's space.*

SARAH: I keep thinking there'll be a knock at the door. And we'll say: Here she is.

KY: Late, as usual.

SARAH: Yes. She'll be thinner.

KY: We'll be tactless about it. I'll say: Good grief, look at her.

SARAH: *(Imagining JANIE in front of them.)* You've lost a little weight Janie.

KY: Have you been sick?

SARAH: She'll say: Thanks a lot, you two.

KY: Then we'll have to make polite chit-chat and courteously refrain from seeming curious until we warm her up.

SARAH: Until she remembers we're old friends who care about her.

KY: Yeah.

SARAH: We'll give her food.

KY: And wine.

Pause.

SARAH: Tell her we've missed her.

Pause.

KY: She'll say: You must think I was crazy.

SARAH: We'll say: No, we don't think that.

KY: She'll apologize about taking your gold ball. She'll say she doesn't know what got into her.

SARAH: I'll say: Oh that's over and done with.

Pause.

KY: It looked like the others.

SARAH: That's how I was fooled.

KY: It's easy to be fooled when you want something to be real.

Pause.

There's something to be said for a humdrum existence. Good old routine. Knowing where you stand.

SARAH: Sometimes we expect too much, and then we're disappointed.

SARAH goes to the window.

I think it's best to live with modest expectations. You can find beauty in—window sills. Or whatever—meets your eye. You can find contentment in friends, in food, a glass of wine. You can find what you need—at hand.

So much disappointment. Where does it come from?

KY: From life.

Scene Thirteen

It's night. JANIE waits by the STATUE. The sky begins to lighten.

As the sun rises, a gold ball rolls onto the pavement.

The LITTLE GIRL enters and retrieves the ball.

LITTLE GIRL: I have a house.

Pause.

JANIE: You?

LITTLE GIRL: Yes, I own a house.

JANIE: Really?

LITTLE GIRL: Yes.

JANIE: And do you live there?

LITTLE GIRL: Of course.

JANIE: Alone?

LITTLE GIRL: No. An old woman keeps the house for me. You

can stay with us if you like. She's very good to me. She gives me things.

JANIE: Is that what you like?

LITTLE GIRL: Of course. She makes me lovely toys.

JANIE: Toys.

LITTLE GIRL: Yes because I am a child.

JANIE: She will not make me toys.

LITTLE GIRL: No, silly. You are grown up. Too old for toys.

JANIE: What will she make for me?

LITTLE GIRL: Nothing, silly. If you live with us, it's your turn to be an old lady—making things for me.

JANIE: I hadn't thought of that.

LITTLE GIRL: Yes. Things to make me happy. And that will make you happy.

JANIE: Does it make the old woman happy?

LITTLE GIRL: Of course.

JANIE: I think I am not old enough.

The LITTLE GIRL exits.

JANIE climbs up to the STATUE.

Hold your hand up to the light.

Look at my hand. All rosy in the light, isn't it? Nearly translucent. See the veins and the shadows of the muscles under the skin?

Do you like my ring?

(*Getting increasingly bitter.*) Feel like you're in church? Looking through a stained glass window? Standing on a cliff watching the sun set over a western sea?

I'll give the ring to you. That way you can give it to someone you care about.

Could you conceivably care about someone?

You are remarkably similar to the statue you were a minute ago. Does that mean you don't change? You can't change? You won't change?

I think you think that's a rhetorical question. But it's not. No, it's not a rhetorical question at all. It's a real, live question. Would you care to tender a real, live answer? Care to be tender?

Tell me what I think? Read my mind?

What's got into you? How often has anything got into you?

Never is a big word. Is never the word you want? What happens in a time called never? Is that the time for putting away childish things?

Or is now the time?

She puts the ring on the STATUE's finger.

She is suspended, frozen.

The WAITER enters and goes to JANIE.

WAITER: You're all right, are you?

You're okay, now? Janie?

He tugs at her arm and gets no response. He rushes off.

TRUE and NORMA enter and stare at JANIE.

The WAITER enters.

WAITER: What do you make of this then?

NORMA walks around JANIE, pokes her a few times.

Look at the way she's staring into his eyes. Gives you the fuckin creeps.

NORMA: Kiss her. In the fairy tales, you'd kiss her. Would he not True? Be a prince and kiss her.

WAITER: No.

NORMA: True, would he not?

WAITER: I've called a doctor.

NORMA: You've called a doctor. So: what did you say? A woman in the square requires destatufication?

WAITER: You're a treat, you are. I said she seems frozen to the spot. And she said: "She'll last till I've had my breakfast, then."

NORMA: Give her a kiss. You don't know if it might not work. Think what a fuckin hero you'd be then. They'd be telling stories of you up and down this coast. Would you not like to be a hero?

WAITER: Oh I would. It would be a cut above being a nonentity.

NORMA: Go on now. Take a chance.

TRUE: Give the woman a fuckin kiss.

WAITER: That'll be the day I'll be taking orders from you True.

NORMA: Do you see True, he knows our names? And it never seemed he did before.

WAITER: I hear you nattering constantly, the two of you, back and forth about your mother and yourselves.

NORMA: Ah, we're just fuckin losers, you know.

WAITER: I'm well aware of that.

NORMA: But you've got the princess here like a block of ice. Go on and see if you can light her fire.

You might do it out of the goodness of your heart. Look at her there. Look at her lips, now, pouting a bit, are they not? Half-open...?

The WAITER climbs up to JANIE. After a moment he kisses her. Stands back. No response.

TRUE: Give her tits a squeeze. I recall that roused me once or twice in me lifetime.

WAITER: Don't be stupid.

NORMA: Were her lips soft?

The WAITER moves off by himself. NORMA prods JANIE again.

TRUE: *(Suddenly interested.)* She's put her ring on his finger.

NORMA: Like a wedding ring, is it? She's gone and wedded herself to the statue.

TRUE: *(Whispering.)* Take it off him. Norma.

NORMA tugs on the ring.

NORMA: *(Whispering.)* It's stuck.

TRUE: Shove over.

TRUE tugs on the ring.

NORMA: It's fuckin stuck.

TRUE tries again.

TRUE: Ah fuck.

NORMA: *(To the WAITER.)* Who's he supposed to be, after all? He's not a saint?

WAITER: How could he be a saint? He's barely decent. He's from some less civilized time. I don't believe he's indigenous. He's Greek maybe. Or Roman.

NORMA: Ah, there's always something sexy about a foreigner.

Did you know I had a man once. I met him the only time I went away. And when I came home, my mother said to me: You're in love with that man whether you know it or not, so you'd better go after him. You won't rest until you've got him.

TRUE: Fuckin send him back. Fuckin drive him out to the head and fuckin dump him in the fuckin sea.

WAITER: What would you do that for?

Pause.

NORMA: For this, for example. Petrifying women.

Can you not picture it?

Down he'd go, fathoms and fathoms down through the lights and shadows of the sea, till he settled in the soft sand at the bottom.

And the soft sand hugged him.

And she'd go after him.

Fall beside him through the water. Lay beside him on the bottom.

TRUE: Till she was bones.

NORMA: But he wouldn't change.

TRUE: He wouldn't change, never.

Pause.

The DOCTOR, an old woman, enters, carrying her bag.

DOCTOR: God love us all, what do we have here on this beauteous morning?

WAITER:	Morning? It's nearly fuckin noon. Did you finish your lunch as well as your breakfast?
NORMA:	She's frozen, Doctor, this one.
DOCTOR:	Come now, be sensible.
WAITER:	Be sensible, she says. Ah, why didn't we all think of that?
DOCTOR:	*(Prodding JANIE.)* Isn't this lovely? Catatonic in the morning.
WAITER:	She'll be catatonic in the afternoon the rate you move.
DOCTOR:	My rate will be another matter.
WAITER:	Don't be looking at me. I'm a poor waiter.
DOCTOR:	Is it these two I'll look to for payment? Ah, nobody's going to pay, is that it?
NORMA:	There's a ring here would pay you—and we'd break the spell and bring her back to life—if we could wrench it from his finger.
DOCTOR:	Bah! She's alive. It's shame's done this to her. The shame of speaking to a statue. The shame of loving and no return. She's alive. Can you not see it in her eyes? Still a flicker in her eyes. Looking into his. And on her lips, there's still signs of salivation.
NORMA:	Ah that'd be the waiter here. Tried to kiss her awake.
WAITER:	Well are you going to do something for God's sake?
DOCTOR:	*(Mysteriously.)* I am. Yes. For I have something in my bag. Something that's sure to do the trick.

She rummages in her bag.

I have something in my bag she'll not be able to resist. Yes. I do have just the thing in my bag guaranteed efficacious in a condition such as this…

She pulls a round, double-sided mirror out of her bag.

Mirror, mirror… Yes. The shock of self-recognition will do the trick, will break the spell—

NORMA: Interrupt her looking at him.

DOCTOR: It's her self that's important, her own self, to look inside herself: *that* will disenchant her.

The DOCTOR holds the mirror up between JANIE and the STATUE.

JANIE doesn't respond.

The STATUE looks into the mirror.

NORMA: The statue moved!

TRUE: It looked into the mirror.

They all look at the STATUE, which is not moving.

WAITER: Ah you're fuckin crazy.

The STATUE looks closer into the mirror.

STATUE: Lookin' good!

Fuck!

Superb. Superior.

Fuck. I feel great.

The STATUE flings his arms out and the ring falls off his finger.

WAITER: What was that?

TRUE: The ring!

TRUE and NORMA go down on their knees looking for the ring.

STATUE: *(To JANIE.)* Hey baby. Feel the wind? Hear the ocean? See the moon?

Sweetie, I have an irresistible desire to be irresistibly desired. And you're just not with it.

NORMA: I found it!

TRUE: I fuckin found it, you fuckin grabbed it out from under my hand.

NORMA: It's mine.

NORMA runs out. TRUE follows her.

STATUE: *(To the WAITER.)* Who are you?

WAITER: Just the waiter.

STATUE: Perfect.

The STATUE exits.

The DOCTOR puts the mirror away and closes her bag. She begins to walk away.

WAITER: Are you leaving her like this?

DOCTOR: I've completed my diagnosis and treatment.

WAITER: She's the same as she was before.

DOCTOR: In this life you often get what you pay for.

WAITER: And often you pay a great deal and get nothing.

The DOCTOR exits.

The WAITER sits on the pedestal, dejected.

I'm a man of few words.

None of them fancy.

Evening falls while he waits, then darkness.

I wish I knew how to wake you.

The sun rises.

No one can know what would wake someone else.

The sun sets.

We already tried many things.

The sun rises.

I guess I should go home.

The sun sets.

I wonder would music work? I could play for you.

The WAITER exits.

Saxophone music floats out over the square.

JANIE awakens and steps down.

Scene Fourteen

In the restaurant. JANIE is sitting at the table just as PAULA left her.

There is a DINER sitting at another table, with his back to JANIE.

PAULA enters. JANIE hides the wallet.

PAULA:	Did you take my wallet?
JANIE:	No.
PAULA:	You didn't see it?
JANIE:	No. There's an old woman around here who steals.
PAULA:	I didn't see any old woman.

JANIE:	Then you must have lost it.

Pause.

Maybe you'd better retrace your steps. Maybe somebody's seen it.

PAULA exits.

The DINER turns to JANIE.

DINER:	I couldn't help hearing your friend was in some distress.
JANIE:	She thought she'd left her wallet.
DINER:	Did she not find it?
JANIE:	No.
DINER:	Ah there's pickpockets in the area and they are smooth.
JANIE:	Smooth.
DINER:	That's right.

JANIE takes PAULA's wallet out of her pocket and sets it on the table.

(*Seductively.*) Like you.

Your friend seemed rather…possessive. Perhaps she erroneously believes in the ownership of people as well as things.

One can own nothing in this life.

You of course know that.

Naked we come into this world and—well.

Pause.

You seem…familiar…

(Very seductively.) What's your name?

JANIE: Myrtle.

DINER: Ah Myrtle. Doesn't it mean victorious?

JANIE: I thought it meant young.

The DINER picks up the wallet and pockets it, smiling.

Scene Fifteen

KY and SARAH's space.

KY: We used to have more fun.

SARAH: We used to have a lot more fun.

KY: We were innocent then.

SARAH: Innocent? Were we?

KY: Oh maybe not. Maybe we were just forgetful.

SARAH: What did we forget?

KY: All the lessons we learned?

SARAH: But you can't live your life if you remember too well. I mean, who'd have a second kid?

KY: *(Happier.)* You're right. With good memories, we'd cut the population in half every generation.

SARAH: *(Happier still.)* If we had to learn from experience, the entire human race would die out.

Scene Sixteen

In the restaurant. JANIE and the DINER have remained sitting.

PAULA returns.

PAULA: Did you take my wallet?

JANIE: No.

PAULA: I've retraced my steps. Nobody's seen it. You didn't see it?

JANIE: No. There's an old woman around here who steals.

PAULA: I didn't see any old woman.

>   *PAULA exits.*
>
>   *The DINER turns to JANIE.*

DINER: I couldn't help hearing your friend was in some distress.

JANIE: She thought she'd left her wallet.

DINER: Did she not find it?

JANIE: No.

DINER: Ah there's pickpockets in the area and they are smooth.

JANIE: Smooth.

DINER: That's right.

(Seductively.) What's your name?

JANIE: Myrtle.

DINER: Ah Myrtle. Does it mean victorious?

JANIE: I thought it meant young. Green, you know. Myrtle grows under the snow in the spring and it's green.

>   *Pause.*

But it might mean victorious.

Scene Seventeen

PAULA returns to the restaurant.

PAULA: Did you take my wallet?

Pause.

JANIE: No. There's an old woman around here who steals.

PAULA: I didn't see any old woman.

Pause.

They look directly at one another.

I know you took it.

Pause.

JANIE: Can I ask you something?

Have you met any of the others?

PAULA: Some.

JANIE: How did you find out about them?

PAULA: *(Correcting.)* Us. How did you find out about *us*.

JANIE: Oh. Yes.

PAULA: People are careless.

JANIE: With one another.

Pause.

There's something I want to tell you. You told me he took from me. You said: he took and took and took.

The problem wasn't that he took from me. The problem was that he didn't.

I would have given more. I had more to give. He didn't want it.

He didn't even see it.

PAULA exits.

Long pause.

JANIE rises and starts to leave.

DINER: Myrtle.

The DINER holds up the wallet.

JANIE: My friend will be back for that. Why don't you hold on to it?

She leaves him sitting there.

The End